SHAKA

A LEGEND OF THE WARRIOR PRINCE

RISING

LUKE W. MOLVER & MASON O'CONNOR

STORY PRESS AFRICA

Published by **Story Press Africa**, an imprint of
Jive Media Africa (South Africa) and **Catalyst Press** (USA).
Website: www.storypressafrica.com

Jive Media Africa

P O Box 22106
Mayor's Walk
3208
South Africa

Tel: +27 33 342 9380/2
Email: admin@jivemedia.co.za
Website: www.jivemedia.co.za

Catalyst Press

2941 Kelly Street
Livermore CA 94551 USA

Tel: 001-925-315-5970
Email: jlpowers@catalystpress.org
Website: www.catalystpress.org

Illustrated by: Luke W. Molver
Written by: Luke W. Molver, Mason O'Connor
Acknowledgement: This work has drawn on *Myth of Iron: Shaka in
History* by Dan Wylie

Library of Congress Control Number: 2017947777

Trade Paper ISBN 978-1-946498-98-4
Trade Cloth ISBN 978-1-946498-99-1

FOREWORD

It is a privilege to have been invited to write the Foreword to this imaginative and innovative presentation of the story of Shaka, the legendary founder of the Zulu Kingdom. The Cambridge Advanced Learner's Dictionary defines legends as very old "stories, not always true, that people tell about a famous event or person." As with all legends, there are numerous accounts of the story of this remarkable ruler. This version synthesizes different accounts of his birth, rejection by his father, years of exile from his people and eventual ascendance to the throne.

The legend of Shaka in the English-speaking world was founded on accounts by white travellers, traders, explorers, missionaries, historians and writers with perspectives and agendas very different from those of the Zulu people. In my work on Southern African Studies, and particularly on Southern African literature written in English, I have focused on Shakan literature; analyzed accounts by black South African and West African writers; and recent historiographic research on the use of oral history as a source of reliable historical information.

The **African Graphic Novel Series** aims to make great African stories accessible to a world-wide audience of young readers, drawing on multiple sources to ensure balanced and credible accounts.

Shaka Rising, the first book in this series, tells Shaka's story with great sensitivity and insight, accompanied by action packed graphics and interesting personal touches that highlight the strengths and weaknesses of various Nguni leaders. It brings history alive to many who would ordinarily not read standard historical accounts. The authors are to be commended for producing an interesting and engaging account of perhaps the best known African monarch in Southern Africa.

Mbongeni Z. Malaba
Professor of English Studies,
University of KwaZulu-Natal
Pietermaritzburg.

THE CHARACTERS
IN "SHAKA RISING"

SHAKA
Son of Senzangakhona
and Nandi

NANDI
Shaka's mother, from
the Langeni

NOMCOBA
Shaka's sister

SENZANGAKHONA
Chief of the Zulu,
Shaka's father

SIGUJANA
Shaka's half-brother,
son of Senzangakhona
and Mbhibhi

NDENGEZI
Friend of Shaka

DINGANE
Shaka's half-brother

IV

ZWIDE
King of the Ndwandwe

DINGISWAYO
King of the Mthethwa

MANANGA
Commander of a Khumalo
ibutho defeated by Zwide,
joins Shaka's forces

JOBE
Chief of the Sithole

MAKHEDAMA
Shaka's cousin, chief
of the Langeni

MBHIBHI
Senzangakhona's favored
wife, mother of Sigujana

MPANDE
Shaka's half-brother

NHLAKA
General of Zwide's forces

THE WORLD OF "SHAKA RISING"

The last part of the 18th century was the time of the American Revolution, the French Revolution, and the expansion of European colonization.

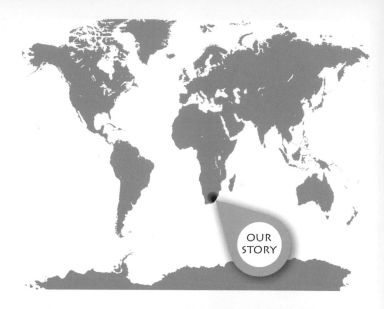

OUR STORY

This was also a time of great turmoil and bloody conflict in south-eastern Africa. The Ndwandwe kingdom, to the north of the Zulu, was expanding its power and territory, attacking neighboring clans and selling them into slavery through the port of Delagoa Bay.

This was the time and region into which Shaka was born, in a small clan surrounded by other chiefdoms vying for control. Through warfare, mediation, and political alliances, Shaka defeated the Ndwandwe and consolidated a new kingdom that has stood to this day.

SOUTHERN AFRICA, LATE 18TH CENTURY...

- - - → Slave trade routes
← ─── Ndwandwe expansion

DELAGOA BAY

Pongola River

Mkhuze River

KHUMALO

White Mfolozi River

Mzinyathi River

NXUMALO

MBOKAZI

NDWANDWE
King Zwide

Black Mfolozi River

INDIAN OCEAN

ZULU
Chief Senzangakhona

SITHOLE
Chief Jobe

Mhlatuze River

LANGENI
Chief Makhedama

MTHETHWA
King Dingiswayo

Thukela River

QWABE

N

Mngeni River

W   E

DURBAN BAY

S

"IT WAS A TIME OF *TURMOIL* IN *AFRICA*... CHIEFDOMS ACROSS THE LANDS BATTLED FOR *SUPREMACY* AMONGST THEMSELVES, WHILE *FOREIGN SHIPS* BROUGHT PALE MEN TO OUR SHORES IN *EVER INCREASING NUMBERS*..."

"... IN SOUTH-EAST AFRICA, *DELAGOA BAY* HAD BECOME A CRUEL CONFLUENCE FOR THE *SLAVE TRADE*, LIKE A *WOUND* IN THE *COASTLINE* ITSELF..."

"... HERE, THE *MOST AVARICIOUS* OF LEADERS WOULD SELL THEIR COUNTRYMEN INTO *CHAINS* FOR THE *GLINT OF COPPER*..."

"... THEY WERE *DARK DAYS*."

"*OUR STORY*, HOWEVER, BEGINS ON THE *DUSTY SAVANNA* OF OUR *OWN LANDS*..."

... SO, THESE BECOME *MY* CATTLE... AND NOW I HAVE THE *MOST*.

THIS IS *UNFAIR!* SHAKA IS *ALWAYS* WINNING... HE *MUST* BE *CHEATING!*

SHAKA, I KNOW TIMES HAVE BEEN DIFFICULT FOR US... EVEN HERE IN OUR OWN HOME WE SOMETIMES FEEL LIKE *OUTCASTS*...

BUT ONE DAY SOON, *SENZANGAKHONA* WILL NAME HIS *SUCCESSOR*...

... AND I HAVE *HIGH HOPES* FOR YOU, MY SON.

YOUR MOTHER *BELIEVES* IN YOU WITH ALL HER HEART... BUT THAT BELIEF *BLINDS* HER TO THE *DANGERS* GROWING AROUND YOU, BROTHER.

I AGREE, *NOMCOBA*...

... EVERY DAY, *SIGUJANA'S MOTHER* SPILLS MORE WHISPERS IN THE CHIEF'S EAR, AND I FEAR THEY HAVE TAKEN *DARK ROOT* IN HIS MIND. HIS EYES HOLD *SUSPICION* AND *PARANOIA* WHEN THEY FALL UPON MY MOTHER AND ME.

5

SEVERAL YEARS LATER, *SHAKA* AND SOME OF THE OTHER ZULU YOUTHS HAD JOINED ONE OF *SENZANGAKHONA'S* YOUNGER REGIMENTS, THE *IWOMBE IBUTHO*...

... WHY MUST WE *TRAIN* SO *CONSTANTLY?* THESE ARE NOT TIMES OF *WAR*...

... YET STILL WE *SHAKE* OUR *SPEARS* AT THE *WIND!*

WE MUST *ALWAYS* BE PREPARED, *DINGANE*, EVEN DURING PEACETIME. LIKE THE *SNAKE* IN THE *GRASS*...

...OUR ENEMIES MAY STRIKE *SUDDENLY* AND *UNEXPECTEDLY!*

WHAT DO *YOU* THINK, *NDENGEZI?* IN THESE MONTHS OF SUMMER, OUR IBUTHO SHOULD BE *DANCING* WITH THE *MAIDENS*, NOT *SPARRING* IN THE *DUST*...

YOU FORGET, *MPANDE*... SENZANGAKHONA HAS *FORBIDDEN* THE WARRIORS OF THE IWOMBE TO TAKE *WIVES*... A DECREE THAT *FRUSTRATES* ME, FOR I HAVE WANTED A *FAMILY* FOR A *LONG TIME*.

7

ELSEWHERE IN THE VILLAGE...

BROTHER, I WORRY MORE EVERY DAY ABOUT *YOUR FUTURE* HERE IN *OUR VILLAGE.*

THE LAST FEW YEARS HAVE SEEN SENZANGAKHONA *CHANGE,* UNDER THE INFLUENCE OF *MBHIBHI...* IT IS CLEAR SHE HAS BECOME HIS *FAVORED WIFE.*

I SEE IT TOO, *NOMCOBA.*

MY MOTHER *NANDI* STILL HOLDS FAST TO MY EARLY YEARS AS THE *SON OF SENZANGAKHONA...*

... BUT SINCE MBHIBHI GAVE HIM *ANOTHER HEIR...*

... *MY PRESENCE* AROUND THE CHIEF'S FIRE SEEMS *DANGEROUSLY UNWELCOME.*

12

YOU WILL BE THE *LEADER* THAT OUR PEOPLE NEED, SHAKA... BUT YOUR TIME HAS NOT YET *COME.* THERE ARE OTHER FEATS TO ACCOMPLISH BEFORE YOU *SIT* IN THE *SEAT* OF A *CHIEF.*

HOWEVER... YOU MUST *LEAVE* THIS VILLAGE TO *ACHIEVE* THOSE GOALS...

... AND I FEAR YOU MUST DO IT *SOON,* FOR YOUR BROTHER *SIGUJANA'S* STARES ARE FILLED WITH MORE *POISON* EVERY TIME HE *LOOKS* AT YOU.

THE INFLUENCE HIS MOTHER HAS OVER THE CHIEF IS *VERY* TROUBLING...

<WHISTLE!>

... DID YOU HEAR THAT?

WHO GOES THERE...?

SHAKA...

... IT IS I, *NDENGEZI.*

13

MY FRIEND, WHY DO YOU APPROACH IN *SECRET* FROM THE *SHADOWS*?

I COME WITH *ALARMING NEWS*, SHAKA... YOUR *LIFE* MAY BE IN *DANGER*.

YOUR BROTHER *SIGUJANA* HAS BEEN SPREADING VENOMOUS LIES ABOUT *YOU* AND YOUR *MOTHER*. YOU HAVE SUPPORTERS AMONG THE *IWOMBE*, BUT SIGUJANA HAS THE *CHIEF'S FAVOR*, AND WITH IT THE SUPPORT OF THE *LARGER REGIMENTS*...

... I BELIEVE HE CONSPIRES TO *HARM* YOU, SHAKA... AND I FEAR YOUR FATHER WILL DO *LITTLE* TO *STOP* HIM.

EVEN IF I *CHALLENGED* SIGUJANA, *MY MOTHER* WOULD STILL BE IN DANGER...

... AND YOU MAY FIND A *COLD IRON SPEARHEAD* IN YOUR *BACK* AS YOU *SLEEP*.

YOU ARE THE ONLY LEGITIMATE THREAT TO SIGUJANA'S *ASCENDANCY* TO THE *ZULU CHIEFTAINSHIP*, SHAKA. I SUSPECT HE WOULD GO TO *ANY LENGTHS* TO *ELIMINATE* SUCH A THREAT.

NOMCOBA IS RIGHT, SHAKA. YOU WILL *ALWAYS* HAVE *FRIENDS* HERE AMONG THE ZULU... BUT FOR NOW, YOU *MUST* *LEAVE*. TONIGHT.

I CAN *HELP* YOU AND YOUR MOTHER GET AWAY *UNNOTICED*... BUT *I* MUST REMAIN HERE. MY DUTY IS STILL TO THE *CHIEF*.

I WILL *STAY*, AND *HELP NDENGEZI*. THE KING HAS NO QUARREL WITH ME... WHERE WILL YOU *GO*, BROTHER?

MY MOTHER HAS FAMILY IN THE *LANGENI* TERRITORIES... MY COUSIN *MAKHEDAMA* RULES THERE. HE WILL GIVE US REFUGE...

PROTECT ONE *ANOTHER*... FOR OUR PEOPLE MAY HAVE A *DIFFICULT PATH* AHEAD.

GOODBYE, MY FRIENDS. I *WILL* SEE YOU AGAIN.

AND SO SHAKA AND HIS MOTHER NANDI *LEFT* THE *ZULU* UNDER COVER OF NIGHT, THE YOUNG WARRIOR CASTING *ONE FINAL GAZE* BACK ON THE *VILLAGE* OF HIS *BIRTH...*

SIGUJANA AND MBHIBHI WOULD BRAND HIM COWARD AND DISHONOR HIS *NAME* AMONG THE *ZULU...* BUT SHAKA KNEW THAT HE MUST SEEK HIS DESTINY *ELSEWHERE* BEFORE HE COULD RETURN TO HIS *OWN* PEOPLE.

UNTIL THEN, THIS *EXILE* WAS THE ONLY WAY TO ENSURE HIS MOTHER'S *SAFETY*, AND HIS *OWN.*

"IT TOOK THE *SON* AND HIS *MOTHER* SEVERAL DAYS TO REACH THE *LANGENI CHIEFDOM,* THE LAND OF *NANDI'S CHILDHOOD...*"

"SHAKA'S COUSIN, *MAKHEDAMA,* NOW RULED THERE... HE AND SHAKA HAD PLAYED TOGETHER AS CHILDREN, BUT HIS WELCOME NOW SEEMED *COLD...*"

"... SHAKA SAW THE FAMILIAR GLINT OF *JEALOUSY* AND *SUSPICION* IN HIS COUSIN'S EYES, AS HE HAD SEEN SO MANY TIMES BEFORE IN THE STARES OF HIS *BROTHER* AND HIS *FATHER*..."

"... AND HE KNEW THAT ONCE AGAIN, HE MUST *LEAVE*."

MOTHER, I DO NOT *BELONG* HERE.

MAKHEDAMA'S DISCOMFORT AROUND ME IS *OBVIOUS*, AND THAT DISCOMFORT WILL ULTIMATELY TURN TO *PARANOIA* IF I REMAIN HERE WITH THE *LANGENI*.

I AM A *WARRIOR*. BUT I MUST FIND A *WORTHY CHIEF* TO ACCEPT MY SPEAR.

I WISH ONLY FOR YOU TO FIND A PLACE OF *BELONGING*, MY SON...

... BUT YOU ARE *MUCH MORE* THAN A WARRIOR. I HAVE KNOWN IT SINCE YOU WERE *BORN*.

THE *PATH* YOU TAKE WILL LEAVE A MARK ON THIS WORLD *FOREVER*.

THEN I MUST *WALK* THAT PATH, MOTHER. AND I MUST WALK IT *ALONE*.

I WILL *RETURN* ONE DAY. UNTIL THEN, YOU WILL BE *SAFE* HERE.

WHERE WILL YOU *GO*, SHAKA?

I WILL SEEK AUDIENCE WITH THE *HIGH KING OF ALL THE SOUTHERN PEOPLES*...

... I WILL OFFER MY SPEAR TO *DINGISWAYO* OF THE MTHETHWA.

"AND ONCE MORE, SHAKA WALKED INTO THE HILLS OF SOUTHERN AFRICA TO CONTINUE HIS JOURNEY, HIS QUEST FOR A *PLACE* OF *BELONGING...*"

"MANY DAYS PASSED AS HE TRAVELED, SETTING HIS FACE EACH MORNING TOWARD THE RISING SUN. HIS DESTINATION WAS THE *MTHETHWA LANDS,* RULED BY *DINGISWAYO,* THE HIGH KING OF ALL THE *CHIEFDOMS* OF THE *SOUTH.*"

"SHAKA KNEW NOT WHAT THE *FUTURE* MIGHT HOLD... BUT HE FELT THE *FLAME* OF HIS *DESTINY* BURN BRIGHTER IN HIS HEART WITH EACH DAY THAT PASSED."

21

OUR FRIENDS IN THE *NXUMALO LANDS* ARE THE MOST RECENT TO FEEL THE SPEARS OF *ZWIDE'S CRUELTY...*

... *HERE,* THEIR HOMESTEADS ARE BEING OVERRUN, THEIR PEOPLE KILLED, OR *CAPTURED* TO SELL AT *DELAGOA BAY...*

... A WISE STRATEGY WOULD BE TO SEND AN IBUTHO TO *AID* THE *NXUMALO.*

MY KING... IF I MAY?

SHOULD THE NXUMALO *FALL,* THE *MBOKAZI PEOPLE* WILL STILL PROVIDE A *BUFFER,* HERE. THE NDWANDWE SEEK *MEN,* NOT LAND, SO IF THE NXUMALO *FLEE...* THE NDWANDWE WILL GIVE *CHASE.*

WE SHOULD RATHER SEND AN IBUTHO TO BOLSTER THE MBOKAZI, *HERE.* ONCE LURED IN BY THE NXUMALO, THE NDWANDWE WILL BE *TIRED* AND *SPENT,* UNPREPARED FOR OUR *AMBUSH.*

I DO NOT *PRESUME* TO *ADVISE*, MY KING, I ONLY—

NO, SHAKA... YOUR INSIGHTS ARE *APPRECIATED*.

YOUR IBUTHO IS THE *STRONGEST*. YOU HAVE PROVEN YOURSELVES IN BATTLE, AND YOUR *LEADERSHIP* HAS EXEMPLIFIED YOUR REGIMENT ABOVE ALL MY OTHERS.

YOUR IBUTHO WILL GO TO AID THE *MBOKAZI*.

IT WILL BE MY *HONOR*, KING DINGISWAYO. I WILL NOT FAIL YOU. I WILL LEAD THE REGIMENT TO *VICTORY* FOR—

YOUR *REGIMENT* WILL AID THE MBOKAZI... BUT YOU WILL *NOT* BE GOING *WITH* THEM, SHAKA.

MY KING... I DON'T *UNDERSTAND*...

YOU HAVE SKILLS *BEYOND* A SIMPLE WARRIOR, MY BOY, AND *ROYAL BLOOD* PUMPS THROUGH YOUR *HEART*.

I WOULD MAKE YOU A *COMMANDER*, AND GIVE YOU *GREATER CONTROL* OVER THE ARMIES OF THE *MTHETHWA*.

SENZANGAKHONA WAS FOOLISH NOT TO *NURTURE* HIS OWN *GARDEN*. BUT YOU HAVE TAKEN *STRONG ROOT* AS THAT *BATTLEFIELD SAPLING*...

... AND YOU WILL *GROW TALL*, YOUR *SHADOW* CAST ACROSS *ENTIRE KINGDOMS*...

HELP ME DEFEAT OUR *ENEMIES*.

TOGETHER WE CAN RESTORE *ORDER* TO OUR LANDS. *POWER* AND *GLORY* WILL BE YOUR REWARD...

"HIS KNOWLEDGE OF *MILITARY TACTICS* AND *LEADERSHIP* GREW QUICKLY, AS DID HIS *RESPECT* WITHIN THE MTHETHWA..."

"... AND DESPITE HIS *YOUTH*, SHAKA SOON BECAME A *TRUSTED ADVISOR* TO KING DINGISWAYO."

"THE SEASONS PASSED, AND AS THE AFTERNOON SKIES SHIFTED THEIR HUE TO THE *BLUE* OF *SPRINGTIME*..."

"... *OTHER FACETS* OF THE YOUNG WARRIOR'S LIFE ALSO CAME *INTO BLOOM*..."

SHAKA... IT APPEARS YOUR **POPULARITY** STRETCHES FURTHER THAN MERELY THE TROOPS UNDER YOUR COMMAND...

KING DINGISWAYO, I AM A **WARRIOR**, MY **FOCUS** WILL **ALWAYS** BE—

MY **BOY!** I AM NOT **SENZANGAKHONA**, I HAVE NO **LAW** FORBIDDING MARRIAGE FOR MY WARRIORS...

... YOU ARE A YOUNG MAN WITH A **GRAND FUTURE** AHEAD OF YOU. YOUR **LEGACY** WILL ECHO ON **DISTANT BATTLEFIELDS**... BUT A **SPEAR** IN ONE'S **HAND** CANNOT COMPARE TO A **MAIDEN** IN ONE'S **ARMS.**

MY KING...YOU **MOCK** ME...

NO, SHAKA. I **HONOR** YOU. AS **YOU** HAVE HONORED ME, WITH GREAT **SERVICE** AND **LOYALTY** THESE PAST MONTHS.

THE **CEREMONY OF FIRST FRUITS** APPROACHES. IT WILL BE A GRAND CELEBRATION, A GATHERING TO **UNITE** ALL THE SOUTHERN PEOPLES AND PLAN FOR THE **FUTURE** OF OUR **NATION.**

I WOULD HAVE **YOU** LEAD THE AMABUTHO IN THE CUSTOMARY WAR DANCE FOR THE GATHERED GUESTS AT OUR VILLAGE. AMONG THE OTHER CHIEFS, YOUR **FATHER** WILL BE WATCHING.

YOU WILL ASK HIM TO HAND YOU YOUR **ASSEGAI**, AND SHOW HIM THAT HERE... **YOU** HOLD RESPECT.

YOU WILL SHOW HIM THE **MAN** THAT HIS **SON** HAS BECOME.

"AS THE *MTHETHWA* PREPARED FOR THE SPRINGTIME CELEBRATIONS, *KING ZWIDE* CONTINUED HIS *SLAVE-RAIDS* ON THE *NORTHERN VILLAGES...*"

"... THE *NDWANDWE FORCES* ROLLED LIKE *WILDFIRE* ACROSS THE SAVANNA, *INESCAPABLE* AND *UNSTOPPABLE.*"

"HOWEVER, THAT *INFERNO* STILL SEEMED *FAR REMOVED* FROM THE RELATIVE *PEACE* OF THE *SOUTHERN LANDS.*"

"DINGISWAYO PREPARED HIS VILLAGE TO HOST THE *FIRST FRUITS CEREMONY,* THE ANNUAL FESTIVAL TO USHER IN *SPRING.* IT WOULD BE A *GATHERING* FOR ALL THE CHIEFDOMS UNDER HIS RULE; HE WOULD *WELCOME* ALL THE CHIEFS AND THEIR PEOPLE AND HOST A GRAND CELEBRATION..."

"... IT WOULD BE A CELEBRATION OF *PEACE* AND *UNITY,* AND *NO BLOODSHED* WOULD BE ALLOWED, REGARDLESS OF INTER-ETHNIC DISPUTES OR *FAMILY FEUDS.*"

"AMONG THE GUESTS ARRIVING AT THE CEREMONY WERE THE *ZULU*, LED BY *CHIEF SENZANGAKHONA* AND PRINCE *SIGUJANA*..."

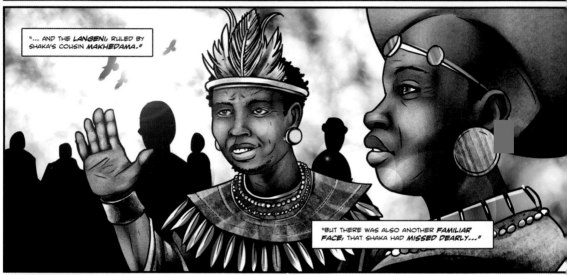

"... AND THE *LANGENI*, RULED BY SHAKA'S COUSIN *MAKHEDAMA*.."

"BUT THERE WAS ALSO ANOTHER *FAMILIAR FACE*, THAT SHAKA HAD *MISSED DEARLY*..."

MOTHER!

SHAKA!

I HAVE *MISSED* YOU.

AND I YOU, MY SON...

29

"AS THE TWO OLD FRIENDS SPOKE, A *HOODED FIGURE* SLIPPED *UNNOTICED* THROUGH THE BUSY VILLAGE..."

"... AND SILENTLY ENTERED *SHAKA'S HUT.*"

"*SHADOWED EYES* FELL UPON HIS *CEREMONIAL ASSEGAI...*"

"... AND THE *PUNGENT STENCH* OF *SMOLDERING HERBS* FILLED THE HUT."

34

36

SHAKA...

SHAKA!

SHAKA, YOU MUST *COME QUICKLY*... KING DINGISWAYO HAS *SUMMONED* YOU *URGENTLY*.

SENZANGAKHONA IS DEAD.

KING DINGISWAYO... *HOW?*

MY MESSENGERS TELL ME HE *FELL ILL* ON THE JOURNEY BACK TO THE ZULU HOME- STEAD. HIS CONDITION *QUICKLY WORSENED*, AND HIS HEALERS AND SANGOMA WERE UNABLE TO HALT THE *CONVULSIONS*... HE BREATHED HIS *LAST* AS THE SUN ROSE.

THE ANCESTORS... *SCORN HIM*. AWAY FROM HIS HOME, CRIPPLED WITH SICKNESS... IT IS *NO WAY* FOR A *WARRIOR* TO *DIE*...

SENZANGAKHONA *HAD* HIS TIME. BUT NOW, SHAKA... IT IS *YOUR TIME.*

TIME TO TAKE YOUR PLACE AS *CHIEF* OF THE *ZULU.*

BUT... *SIGUJANA...*

SIGUJANA IS A *SPOILED CHILD* WHO WILL RULE THE ZULU AS A *PETTY TYRANT.* HIS CLAIM IS SUPPORTED ONLY BECAUSE THE PEOPLE HAVE NO OTHER *VIABLE CANDIDATE* TO RALLY BEHIND...

... BUT *YOU,* SHAKA.

THE ZULU WILL *REMEMBER* THE EVENTS OF THE FIRST FRUITS CEREMONY. THEY WITNESSED YOUR FATHER *ACKNOWLEDGE YOU,* AND YOU MAY CLAIM THIS RIGHT TO *CHALLENGE* YOUR BROTHER SIGUJANA.

YOUR PEOPLE NEED NOT ONLY A *STRONG* LEADER, BUT ONE WHO POSSESSES BOTH *CUNNING* AND *CHARISMA...*

... *YOU* ARE THAT *LEADER,* SHAKA.

WITH YOU AT THE HEAD OF THE ZULU, WE WILL LEAD OUR NATION INTO A NEW AGE OF *PROSPERITY.*

"WHATEVER *EMOTIONS* SHAKA FELT OVER HIS *FATHER'S DEATH* WERE QUICKLY *BURIED* BENEATH THE LANDSLIDE OF *LOOMING WAR*..."

"... AND A *LOVE* ONLY *BEGINNING* TO *BLOSSOM* WAS *CUT SHORT* BY THE *POLITICS* OF AN *EMPIRE*."

"SO, AT THE HEAD OF DINGISWAYO'S *FINEST AMABUTHO*, SHAKA MARCHED FOR THE *LANDS* OF THE *ZULU*... THE LANDS HE ONCE CALLED *HOME*."

42

... *SHAKA,* OUR FORCES WOULD BE STRONGER HERE IF THE LANGENI WERE TO PLEDGE THEIR SPEARS TO US...

THE LANGENI WARRIORS SUFFER FROM *POOR TRAINING,* BUT THEIR SKILLS CAN BE SHARPENED BY THE *IRON* OF THE *ZULU...*

... *MOTHER,* WHAT DO YOU THINK? WOULD *MAKHEDAMA* GIVE ME HIS ALLEGIANCE AS SENZANGAKHONA'S SUCCESSOR?

I BELIEVE SO, MY SON. YOUR COUSIN HAS TREATED YOU *DISRESPECTFULLY* BEFORE...

BUT MAKHEDAMA IS A *FOLLOWER,* NOT A *LEADER.* NOW THAT YOU ARE CHIEF OF THE ZULU, HE WILL *SEEK* YOUR *FAVOR.*

THAT IS *GOOD NEWS...* BUT IT IS STILL *NOT ENOUGH.* WE NEED MORE TROOPS IF WE ARE TO *DEFEAT ZWIDE.*

DINGISWAYO HAS BECOME *CARELESS,* FOCUSING ONLY ON THE NEXT *MAIDEN* HE *BEDS* AND *NEGLECTING* THE *AFFAIRS OF STATE.*

THEN IT IS *MORE* THAN TROOPS WE NEED, SHAKA... IT IS *LEADERSHIP*.

I AM YOUR *CHIEF*, BUT *DINGISWAYO* IS STILL YOUR *KING*. YOU WOULD DO WELL TO *REMEMBER* THAT, NDENGEZI.

WARRIORS ARRIVED AT OUR GATES THIS MORNING. THEY ARE LED BY *MANANGA* OF THE *KHUMALO* PEOPLE, FROM FAR TO THE NORTH...

HIS *SKILLS* ON THE *BATTLEFIELD* ARE WELL-KNOWN... AND *I* TOO UNDERSTAND WHAT IT IS TO BE A *LEADER* OF *LOST WARRIORS*.

I WILL SPEAK WITH MANANGA... AND PUT HIS *REPUTATION* TO THE *TEST*.

MOTHER, IF YOU WOULD ACCOMPANY ME...

HE HAS BECOME... *HARDER*. LIKE THE HIDE OF A SHIELD, STIFFENING IN THE SUN.

HE *HAS* TO BE TOUGH, NOMCOBA. AS THE *SHIELD* OF OUR *PEOPLE*, HE MUST DRAW STRENGTH FROM THIS *NEW DAY'S SUN*...

... BECAUSE THE *DARKNESS* IS COMING.

YOU ARE *KHOMFIYA*. THE TALES OF YOUR SKILLS AS A WARRIOR ARE *IMPRESSIVE*. BUT WHERE IS YOUR *IBUTHO?*

NKOSI SHAKA... WE SUFFERED *HEAVY LOSSES* AGAINST THE *NDWANDWE*. THEY MOVE LIKE AN *INFECTION* ACROSS THE LANDS OF THE NORTH...

... AND WHEN NEWS OF *SENZANGAKHONA'S PASSING* REACHED US, I FEARED THINGS WOULD *WORSEN* FOR THE *ZULU PEOPLE*.

WHY DID YOU THINK *THAT*, KHOMFIYA?

SIGUJANA'S REPUTATION WAS... *POOR*, NKOSI.

BUT WHEN I LEARNED THAT IT WAS *YOU* WHO HAD ASCENDED TO THE THRONE OF THE ZULU, MY *HOPES* WERE *LIFTED* FOR THE SOUTHERN PEOPLES. I GATHERED WHAT REMAINED OF MY *IBUTHO*, AND MADE THE TREK HERE...

THEN YOU *FLED* YOUR BATTLES, KHOMFIYA?

NO, KING SHAKA...! OUR HONOR WOULD *NEVER ALLOW* US SUCH *COWARDICE*... WE CAME TO OFFER OUR SPEARS TO YOU, TO BOLSTER YOUR FORCES AND TAKE THE *OFFENSIVE* AGAINST *ZWIDE*—

"... I REMEMBER THAT NIGHT."

VICTORY... IS *YOURS*, BROTHER.

AS IS THE *LEADERSHIP* OF THE *ZULU*... A BURDEN THAT PROVED *TOO HEAVY* FOR *MY SHOULDERS*..

PERHAPS... YOU *ARE* THE *CHIEF* OUR PEOPLE *NEED*, SHAKA.

GOODBYE, SIGUJANA.

BUT IT IS *ANOTHER NIGHT* THAT MY THOUGHTS DWELL ON, NOMCOBA. MANY YEARS AGO... THE EVENING I LEFT OUR *HOME*...

... WE SAT IN THE DARKNESS OF MY MOTHER'S HUT, RIGHT *THERE.* I EXPRESSED MY *FEARS* ABOUT MY *FUTURE* AMONG THE ZULU, AND THE *EXPECTATIONS* OF NANDI AND SENZANGAKHONA...

YOU COUNSELED ME *WELL*, MY SISTER. I REMEMBER YOUR WORDS; YOUR ADVICE ABOUT THE *PATH* THAT LAY AHEAD.

"THERE ARE OTHER FEATS TO ACCOMPLISH *BEFORE* YOU SIT IN THE SEAT OF A CHIEF."

I DID NOT *FULLY APPRECIATE* THOSE WORDS THEN, BUT THEY HAVE *REMAINED* WITH ME...

I STILL *LEARN* FROM THOSE WORDS *EVERY DAY.* BECAUSE EVERY DAY THERE IS *MORE* TO ACCOMPLISH. ANOTHER *CLAN* I MUST BRING UNDER MY *WING*.

ANOTHER *ALLIANCE* TO *FOSTER.*

ANOTHER *ENEMY* TO *CRUSH.*

AND I ASK MYSELF, WILL THESE TASKS EVER *CEASE?*

BUT I KNOW, THEY WILL *NOT.* FOR IT IS NOT ONLY THE *PATH* OF A CHIEF THAT IS PAVED WITH SUCH TASKS...

... IT IS THE *ROLE* OF A CHIEF.

I MAY NOT HAVE ADMITTED IT TO MYSELF ALL THOSE YEARS AGO... BUT I HAVE *ALWAYS* BEEN A CHIEF, NOMCOBA.

IT IS NOT *ARROGANCE;* IT IS THE REALIZATION OF MY *RESPONSIBILITY* TO OUR PEOPLE.

IT IS THE KNOWLEDGE THAT I MUST MAKE *DIFFICULT DECISIONS,* THAT WILL AFFECT THOSE I *CARE* ABOUT...

WHEN THE NEW MOON RISES, YOU WILL *MARRY* MAYANDEWA OF THE MTHETHWA.

THIS WILL SOLIDIFY RELATIONS WITH HIS CLAN, A SMALL BUT STRATEGICALLY PLACED AREA THAT WILL BE ADVANTAGEOUS IN OUR BATTLES AGAINST THE NDWANDWE.

NKOSI YAMI... *MY BROTHER...* PLEASE, I DO NOT *LOVE* MAYANDEWA --

I DO NOT MAKE THESE DECISIONS *LIGHTLY,* NOMCOBA. AND I AM NOT BLIND TO THE *FEELINGS* OF THOSE AROUND ME... BUT I CANNOT SEND TROOPS AGAINST *ALL* MY RIVALS. *DIPLOMACY* MUST BE *RESPECTED....* AND YOUR *MARRIAGE* TO *MAYANDEWA* WILL MAKE OUR COMBINED PEOPLES MORE POWERFUL.

BUT... *NDENGEZI...*

DO NOT FORGET, THAT BEFORE I AM YOUR BROTHER... I AM *YOUR CHIEF.*

THIS IS MY WILL.

... AND *SHAKA'S WILL* WOULD SHAPE THE ZULU DESTINY FOR *YEARS* TO COME... AN *IRON WILL,* SHARP AS THE HEAD OF AN ASSEGAI, THAT WOULD NOT *BEND OR BREAK....* BUT WOULD *CUT* ALL THOSE CLOSE TO HIM, *FRIEND* AND *FOE* ALIKE...

NOMCOBA SAW THE *CHANGE* IN HER BROTHER, BUT SHE UNDERSTOOD HIM BETTER THAN MOST... AND KNEW THAT SHE MUST *FULFIL* HER ROLE AS A *PRINCESS* OF THE *ZULU.*

"THOUGH HIS MIND WAS WEIGHTED WITH *HEAVY THOUGHTS*, SHAKA TOOK *NO RESPITE* FROM HIS DUTIES. THE ZULU STILL NEEDED MORE TROOPS TO ADEQUATELY DEFEND AGAINST *ZWIDE'S FORCES*..."

"... AND WHERE HE COULD NOT GAIN THE ALLEGIANCE OF NEIGHBORING TRIBES WITH AN *OPEN HAND*... SHAKA WOULD USE A *CLENCHED FIST*."

SHAKA... THE *SITHOLE FORCES* NUMBER *GREATER* THAN WE ANTICIPATED...

THE SITHOLE HAVE NOT FELT THE MIGHT OF THE *ZULU AMABUTHO*... *ONE* OF OUR WARRIORS IS WORTH *TEN* OF THEIRS, AND THEIR CHIEF *JOBE* IS OLD AND FEEBLE!

BE *CAUTIOUS* WITH YOUR *CONFIDENCE*, MANANGA. IT CAN QUICKLY TURN TO *PRIDE* IN YOUR MOUTH... AND ENTIRE *EMPIRES* HAVE BEEN *POISONED* BY SUCH *SWEET NECTAR*.

"... LET US SHOW THESE SITHOLE HOW THE ZULU FIGHT!"

"AND SO AS THE BATTLE AGAINST THE SITHOLE BEGAN, THE CHIEF OF THE ZULU WANDERED ITS OUTSKIRTS, *ALONE*, AND DEEP IN *CONTEMPLATION*."

"SHAKA HAD GREAT TRUST IN HIS COMMANDERS, BUT FELT HIMSELF WEARIED BY THE *ENDLESS POLITICS* AND *BATTLES* OF *RULERSHIP*; BURDENED BY HIS OWN *UNCOMPROMISING DECISIONS*. HE KNEW HIS JOURNEY WAS NOT OVER, AND MANY TRIALS STILL AWAITED HIM..."

"... THE MANTLE OF LEADERSHIP *HUNG HEAVY* ON HIS SHOULDERS."

"AS THE SOUNDS OF DISTANT BATTLE ROSE ABOVE THE SAVANNA, SHAKA SAW A *LONE FIGURE* SITTING ATOP THE HILLSIDE AHEAD..."

AND I... MERELY A *WANDERER*, MUSING ON THE *POLITICS* OF *WAR*.

NKOSI SHAKA! THE SITHOLE HAVE OVERWHELMED US... WE MUST RETREAT!

YOU RECOGNIZE ME NOW, *JOBE*.

I KNEW WHO YOU WERE WHEN YOU WALKED UP THE HILL, *SHAKA*. BUT I WANTED TO SPEAK TO YOU, TO GAIN YOUR *MEASURE* AS A *MAN*... NOT A *CHIEF*.

AND WHAT HAS THAT MEASURE *SHOWN YOU*?

IT HAS SHOWN ME *ENOUGH*.

TAKE YOUR REMAINING TROOPS, *SHAKA*. *WITHDRAW* FROM THE BATTLEFIELD WITH *DIGNITY*, MY FORCES WILL *NOT* STOP YOU.

AND NEXT TIME WE MEET... WE CAN CALL EACH OTHER *ALLIES*.

"AND SO SHAKA'S *LOSS* AGAINST THE SITHOLE THAT DAY *HUMBLED* HIM, BUT ALSO GAVE HIM FURTHER *INSIGHT* INTO THE WAYS OF RULERSHIP... AND ULTIMATELY, A *NEW* AND *VALUABLE* ALLY IN *JOBE*."

61

"MEANWHILE, IN THE *MTHETHWA HOMESTEAD,* THE ELDERS WERE *CONCERNED* ABOUT THEIR *KING...* DINGISWAYO *NEGLECTED* HIS DUTIES AS RULER, IN A TIME WHEN HIS PEOPLE NEEDED *STRONG LEADERSHIP* MORE THAN *EVER.*"

"HIS *NEW BRIDE,* A BEAUTIFUL MAIDEN WHO HAD *FLED* THE SLAVE RAIDS IN THE *NORTH,* SEEMED TO BE DINGISWAYO'S *ONLY* FOCUS..."

"SHE WOULD TAKE THE KING ON *LONG WALKS* OUTSIDE THE VILLAGE, WHILE THE PEOPLE *SLEPT...*"

"... AND ONE NIGHT, *DARK FIGURES* AWAITED THEM BENEATH THE *JAGGED MOON.*"

DINGISWAYO...

"... BUT THAT IS A STORY FOR ANOTHER EVENING...."

THE STORY
CONTINUES

By uniting the people in a land rife with turmoil and unrest, Shaka established himself as a leader for the people. Through his tactics and political awareness, he turned the humble Zulu chiefdom into the great Kingdom of the Zulu.

Today, Shaka's legacy lives on. The land was established as "KwaZulu" – country of the Zulu – and is now one of South Africa's nine provinces: KwaZulu-Natal. The Zulu monarchy is recognized by the state, and is currently under the rule of King Goodwill Zwelithini, a descendant of Shaka. More than 12 million people identify themselves as Zulu, constituting almost a quarter of South Africa's population, making it the largest ethnic group in South Africa.

All of this was set in motion when Shaka defeated Zwide's men, consolidating his leadership. However, this was merely the beginning of his reign, which would see more politics, warfare, and family feuds, as well as strange new pale-skinned men... and he had not seen the last of the Ndwandwe either.

HOW CAN WE BE SURE THAT THIS STORY IS ACCURATE?

Shaka Rising is a "historical fiction." Based in fact, as far as possible, it is merely one "telling" of the story; but other versions do exist. Because no written form of language existed in the Zulu culture at that time, all the history of the Zulu people was retained in the telling of stories. It was not until Europeans arrived later on that details of Zulu culture were recorded in ink for the first time. These written records mostly reflect the perspectives of the European writers.

Both the oral history and the written records can prove to be sketchy. In the telling of stories, one might exaggerate, either to impress or to portray one's position in the story favorably. As these stories get passed down from generation to generation, each telling more embellished than the last, we may end up with a story bearing little resemblance to the truth. And when these stories are passed down by different people with different motives, we can end up with two completely different stories.

The written records, although not so easily altered by the "broken telephone," were often no more accurate, as they were not subject to much scrutiny, and the writers had their own agendas. The historical record about the Shaka period has left us with documents mostly authored by Europeans. In the past, these were taken at face value, as historical fact. If we inspect them more closely, however, we find that there is little evidence to support the version of the story they

AND SO SHAKA AND HIS MOTHER NANDI **LEFT** THE **ZULU** UNDER COVER OF NIGHT, THE YOUNG WARRIOR CASTING **ONE FINAL GAZE** BACK ON THE **VILLAGE** OF HIS **BIRTH**...

SEE PAGE 15

contain. Such is the case with a number of writings on Shaka. The absolute truth of what happened is, therefore, as much a legend as Shaka himself. The best one can do is look at all available records, and come to one's own conclusions of what most likely happened.

SEE PAGE 25

One contentious issue, for example, is that of Shaka's initial departure from the Zulu. In this version of the story, Shaka is seen to be quite old already before he leaves, and he leaves of his own accord. Others say that he and his mother were, in fact, banished by Senzangakhona while Shaka was still a child.

There are also aspects of Shaka's life for which very few records exist at all, and some elements of the story have been fabricated in *Shaka Rising* for the sake of exploring "what might have been." Nobuhle, for example, was made up to explore Shaka's romantic life. However, the truth is that very few accounts of Shaka's life include any sort of woman partner.

THE HISTORICAL SETTING OF SHAKA'S STORY

Shaka Rising takes place in the late 18th and early 19th centuries. Shaka was born sometime in the 1780s–the date varies according to the source. The United States of America had just gained independence from British rule after the American Revolution. The French Revolution would soon follow, around the time of Shaka's childhood. Australia had just been "discovered" by the British, who would soon establish their first settlement there. The Ottoman Empire was on the decline, following a period of peace in which their military prowess had been overtaken by that of their rivals. Their influence in the trade routes between East and West became less significant with the establishment of a ship route via the Cape of Good Hope.

SEE PAGE 2

CHIEFTAINSHIPS OF THE ZULU

Zulu kaMalandela, founder of the clan

Gumede kaZulu

Phunga kaGumede

Mageba kaGumede (c.1667–c.1745), son of Gumede chief of the Zulu clan from c.1727–c.1745

1488   1652   ±1667

EVENTS IN WORLD HISTORY

Sea route to the East via Cape of Good Hope

Dutch establish a settlement at the Cape of Good Hope

At the Cape of Good Hope (now Cape Town), the British had just taken over rule from the Dutch, and tensions were high. At Delagoa Bay (now Maputo), trading posts had been established for trade with the local peoples.

Among the items traded were things like ivory, copper, and, of course, slaves. Typically, chiefs of the area would sell their prisoners of war as slaves for a good profit. In response to an expanding slave trade, predominantly for plantation labor in South America, slavers escalated their raids on chiefdoms and villages to capture prisoners, who were then sold as slaves.

SEE PAGE 6

The Zulu were a small clan living approximately 200 km north-east of the present-day port of Durban. The time line shows the successive chiefs of the Zulu in relation to some major historical events elsewhere in the world.

..a kaMageba, son of Mageba, chief of the Zulu clan from c.1745- 1763

Jama kaNdaba (c.1757–1781), son of Ndaba, chief of the Zulu clan from 1763–1781

Senzangakhona kaJama (c.1762–1816), son of Jama, chief of the Zulu clan from 1781–1816

Sigujana kaSenzangakhona, son of Senzangakhona, chief of the Zulu clan c.1816

Shaka becomes chief of the Zulu, c.1816

..5   ±1757   ±1762 1776   1789   1806   1815 ±1816 ±1816   1833

American Declaration of Independence

French Revolution

British take control of the Cape of Good Hope

End of the Napoleonic Wars in Europe

Abolition of slavery in Britain

ZULU POLITICAL STRUCTURES

Shaka's rise to power is often understood as a dramatic example of state-building, contrasted with the earlier, more localized, clan-based systems of power organized around homesteads of extended family groups. As chiefs began to consolidate their power in the late 18th century, they were able to demand tribute and taxes from the people they ruled through a web of social, political, and economic obligations, backed by military power. Shaka is best known for conquering neighboring chiefdoms, and uniting them into one organized kingdom under his leadership. He was able to command and extract labor from young men for both military service and building projects. In return, he offered protection and helped to resolve disputes.

SEE
PAGE
59

SHAKA AS A LEADER

... THE TROOPS *CHANT* HIS *NAME* AS A *BATTLE-CRY*...

SHA-KA!

SEE PAGE 19

PATH TO LEADERSHIP

Shaka lived in a patriarchal society, in which the position of chief was handed down from father to son. But what did it take to be chosen as the son to whom the position would be passed down? Shaka was favored amongst the people to be the next chief, due to a combination of intelligence, skill as a warrior, and natural charisma.

This counted for little, however, when the mother of his half-brother Sigujana persuaded his father that Sigujana should be the next chief of the Zulu.

SEE PAGE 11

I WOULD MAKE YOU A *COMMANDER*, AND GIVE YOU *GREATER CONTROL* OVER THE ARMIES OF THE *MTHETHWA*.

But King Dingiswayo admired Shaka's traits and chose Shaka to be commander of his army.

To become chief of the Zulu, Shaka had to eliminate the competition by killing his brother. Finally, when Dingiswayo died, the paramount Mthethwa kingdom fell into disarray, and there was chaos as all the constituent clans looked for protection from the looming Ndwandwe. Shaka once again eliminated the competition, and then had to form strategic alliances to establish himself as the new king.

SEE PAGE 23

When we look at this story, we begin to see how important the circumstances and context are in determining new leaders. Shaka became chief partly because he was physically able to defeat his competition in battle. In modern times, this would have counted for little. His intelligence and charisma, however, would still count for a lot.

SEE PAGE 55

YOU COUNSELED ME *WELL*, MY SISTER. I REMEMBER YOUR WORDS, YOUR *ADVICE* ABOUT THE *PATH* THAT LAY AHEAD.

"THERE ARE OTHER FEATS TO ACCOMPLISH BEFORE YOU SIT IN THE SEAT OF A CHIEF."

ROLE OF A LEADER

What does it mean to be a leader? Is it social status? A job? A position of authority? Is it being the person who gets to make all the decisions? If so, why can everybody not just make their own decisions? Throughout history, humans have lived in groups, and those groups have had leaders. The Zulu had a chief. The Mthethwa had a king. Even today, we see that countries have presidents, companies have CEOs, sports teams have captains. So, what exactly is the role of a leader?

INDEED... **BLOOD** WILL SOAK THE GROUND BEFORE THE NIGHT FALLS TODAY. A **PITY...** THE SOUTHERN NATIONS WOULD BE STRONGER **UNITED**, INSTEAD OF **SPLIT** WITH **INFIGHTING**.

SEE PAGE 60

At different stages in the story, Shaka has different leadership roles to play. He leads his people into battle, forges alliances with other clans, and protects his people from the attacks of Zwide. This required tactical thinking and decisiveness, but it also required trust from the people. Being a leader carries with it authority, which is necessary when making decisions for a group. But authority can be abused. In *Shaka Rising*, we see a number of characters who are not just leaders, but rulers–each with their own characteristics and traits: Senzangakhona, Dingiswayo, Zwide, Jobe, and, of course, Shaka. Look at how each of them acts in leadership roles, and you begin to get an idea of the difference between "ruling" and "leading."

ZULU SOCIAL STRUCTURES

THE ROLE OF WOMEN

Shaka Rising took place within the setting of a patriarchal society, in which men hold power and authority over women and children. This has been a common societal construct throughout history, and south-eastern Africa was no different. This said, women in the Zulu culture were not necessarily seen as inferior. Men were the head of the household, but women were not less pivotal; everybody had their part to play.

The Zulu culture also allowed for men to have a number of wives. Traditionally, the acquisition of more wives would be initiated by the first wife, so she could have more help with the daily chores.

The day-to-day role of women included all the general chores of running a household, including growing the crops, preparing the food, fetching the water and cleaning the house.

NANDI! GO AND FETCH MORE WATER! AND TAKE **SHAKA** WITH YOU!

SEE PAGE 5

The most essential role of women was to raise the children: watching over them, teaching them their duties, and disciplining them. All the women of a homestead were responsible for the children.

Regardless of biological parentage, all children called each other "brother" and "sister," and all women were regarded as "Mom." The women would also be the ones to tell the children stories, an important part of Zulu culture.

VERY WELL... GATHER ROUND CHILDREN, FOR *THAT* STORY IS PART OF *ALL* OUR STORIES...

SEE PAGE 1

Women were not without rank in society, either. The grandmother of the family was highly respected.

Other "highly ranked" women, such as the chief's wives, held considerable influence, too

Some were even consulted as advisors, such as how Shaka consulted his mother.

Women were also used as political devices. A chief might give his daughter or his sister to another chief as a gift to strengthen relations, or to become married into another family to create family ties and form alliances between chiefdoms.

... I WOULD SEEK FURTHER COUNSEL WITH *MY WIFE.*

SEE PAGE 11

BROTHERS AND SISTERS

SIGUJANA
Shaka's half-brother

NOMCOBA
Shaka's sister

In this story, we meet a few of Shaka's siblings, namely Sigujana and Nomcoba, as well as Dingane and Mpande, who play an important role later in Zulu history. They were all what we today call half-siblings: they shared a father but had different mothers.

If you have any siblings, you will likely be familiar with the close bonds that you form, as well as the rivalries that occur. Shaka and Sigujana grew up together, much as brothers today would.

However, despite their history, there came a time when one brother killed the other.

SEE PAGE 42

DINGANE
Shaka's half-brother

MPANDE
Shaka's half-brother

SEE PAGE 40

By today's standards, this would be seen as extreme. So, was Shaka heartless, or is this merely a reflection of the contrasting circumstances between then and now? The killing of family members sometimes occurred to eliminate rivals in an individual's path to sovereignty. Does this mean that the bond between siblings was less important than it is considered now?

Compare this with the relationship he had with Nomcoba. The two trusted and cared for each other.

Shaka did give her away to a man she did not love, but it was no easy task for him. There was still a bond between them.

SEE PAGE 25

Families and Communities

Families would live in a ring of huts around a central cattle enclosure. The father, head of the family, would occupy the main hut at the top of the circle, and each wife and her children would have a hut either side of his. While the women tended to the daily chores, the boys would look after the livestock. Once old enough, boys would have to join an "ibutho", a regimented unit who were trained as warriors as well as performing labor tasks required by the chief. The boys would then move off to start families of their own nearby.

The exact way in which these families fitted together in political spheres is unclear. At the time of Shaka's birth, the Zulu were a small chiefdom that existed under the paramount Mthethwa kingdom. So, what did it mean to be

Zulu? Was it a question of lineage? Or living in a particular geographical location? Or having sworn allegiance to the chief? Furthermore, how did this fit into the paramount kingdom? Senzangakhona was a chief in his own right, who commanded the military power and had authority in his community. But he would answer to Dingiswayo's call as the king of the Mthethwa.

What does that say about the interactions and relationships between different chiefdoms? The only written records are those of the few European traders who passed through, subject to their Western interpretations of these different cultures and social structures. They knew little about these, especially since they were unable to understand the Zulu language. Without any reliable records, it is very difficult to say with any certainty how these communities functioned politically.

Aspects of Zulu culture

Cattle And Wealth

Cattle were the most important indication of a man's wealth and status. They were slaughtered and eaten as part of ceremonial rituals on special occasions such as weddings and funerals and also as a means to appease the ancestors in times of trauma and hardship.

Lobola ("bride-price") was a payment in cattle made by the groom to the father of the bride. Cattle were also used as currency for trading.

Cattle hide was used to make things such as garments and shields, and the horns were used as ivory.

AND WHY WOULD I NEED MORE **SPEARS** IN THIS **SUMMER PEACETIME,** BOY? IT IS **CATTLE** THAT HOLD VALUE THIS SEASON, AND YOU HAVE BROUGHT **NONE OF THOSE** TO MY VILLAGE...

SEE PAGE 10

BEADS: COLORFUL SIGNALS

Glass beads were an integral part of Zulu culture. Different colors came to mean different things, and one would adorn oneself in an arrangement of colors for certain purposes.

A woman looking for a husband might have worn predominantly red to show fertility. She would also have worn colors chosen for her by her father to show lineage. Women also wore beads to show wealth, and they used them as a form of currency.

HEADDRESS AND STATUS

Commanders and chiefs would wear a crown of feathers to show authority, also usually adorned with certain beads and animal skins to show such things as lineage.

The traditional headdress of women was worn after they were married, or old enough to warrant respect.

BELIEFS

Belief in the supernatural was a significant aspect of Zulu culture. The ancestors of an individual and his or her clan played an important role in how Zulu people understood health and managed daily and relational conflict. Illness was broadly defined, and restoring peace within families, clans, and communities was part of managing personal and communal health. Diviners, called "izangoma," (singular: isangoma) sought help and wisdom from their ancestors and the ancestors of their patients, by throwing ceremonial bones and other objects, from which they would divine the future by the way in which they landed. Izangoma could diagnose illness, grant favorable conditions, wish ill upon another person, solve and/or create conflicts within relationships. Patients also consulted izangoma for protection from a variety of disasters such as lightning or evil spirits.

Patients further consulted herbalists, called "izinyanga." An inyanga used plants and animals to prepare medicines, known as "umuthi," to be applied to people or things for similar reasons – to cure illness, to seek health or good luck, or to curse or poison one's personal enemies. Early European travelers and settlers struggled to understand African systems of medicine, particularly as they appeared to conflict with Christian knowledge and belief systems, and European biomedical doctors and Zulu healers clashed and struggled against each other. Yet today, Zulu "traditional" healers remain an important part of a complicated medical landscape as modern Zulus continue to consult izangoma and izinyanga for a variety of illnesses and personal problems alongside their biomedical counterparts.

HOWEVER, YOUR BONES DO NOT REVEAL *EVERYTHING,* SANGOMA, FOR IT IS *NOT SIGUJANA* WHO WILL BE LEADING THE ZULU...

SEE PAGE 44

LANGUAGE

The dialect that was spoken at the time was common throughout most of the clans. This language has come to be known as isiZulu, the language of the Zulu.

Many Zulu words contain click sounds. In writing these are recorded by using the letters 'c', 'q', and 'x'. The sound represented by 'x' is made by sucking your tongue away from the inside of your cheek.

... YET STILL WE *SHAKE* OUR *SPEARS* AT THE *WIND!*

SEE PAGE 7

IsiZulu is a descriptive language. Words are commonly based on the sound of what they are describing. For example, there is a town called Ixopo which is close to wetlands. When you pronounce the name "Ixopo" it sounds like the hoof of a cow or horse walking in the mud

The language also makes use of many idioms. Instead of saying, "We have no enemies to fight," one might have said, "We shake our spears at the wind."

A popular custom was that of praise poetry, which made extensive use of idioms. The praise poet would sing the chief's "praises" as a form of entertainment. Senzangakhona, for example, was called "The one who is fat even in the time of famine." To be fat during a famine would suggest he was a self-serving chief.

Shaka was said to be "The one whose fame spreads even while he is seated."

QUESTIONS AND IDEAS FOR GOING DEEPER

The way in which the material in this book is organised uses the following pattern:
- You start by reading (and viewing) the story just as it is.
- Next, there are questions and ideas to help you get a deeper understanding of what you have read.
- Finally, you think about how this applies to life as you know it (your own life, or the world in which you live).

You have read the story of Shaka as a boy and young man. In the notes and questions on pages 69-87 you have focused in more detail on particular aspects of Shaka's life The questions which follow will challenge you to think about what Shaka's life has to do with yours: What is different? What is the same? What have you learned from reading his story?

CRITICAL THINKING QUESTIONS

How accurate is this story? How do we know?
- In what other ways might the history have been skewed?
- What other instances throughout the world do you think might have been subject to fabricated history?
- Do you think it is likely that Shaka would have had a relationship with a woman, or do you think there would have been more accounts of it if he had?

The history of Shaka's time
- What was going on in other parts of the world at that time?
- How did the events at Delagoa Bay shape what happened in the story?
- How did the events in the story help shape history up to the present day?

Shaka as a leader

● To what extent do leadership positions exist today in the same social structures as in the story?

● Think about some of the leaders in society today. What are their roles and how were they chosen?

● Think about the leaders of some groups that you may have been in (sports team captain, school cheer leader, etc.). What are the roles of those positions? Were the ways in which they were chosen suitable for the positions, or could they have been done a different way?

The role of women

● Think about the role that women play in the society in which you live. In what ways is it different to that of the women in this story?

● Are the roles of women changing in our modern society? How so, and why?

Brothers and sisters

● When we compare the relationships between siblings in the story with those in our own society, what does it bring to light about the meaning we hold for the labels of "brother" and "sister"?

Social structures

● To what extent do you think this telling of the story resonates with how the characters themselves would have interpreted the situation in the context of their own culture?

● To what extent do you think the idea of a royal bloodline, such as the Zulus, was an attempt by European writers to align what they observed with their preconceived notion of monarchy, based on Western culture?

GLOSSARY

assegai
short stabbing spear
used by Zulu warriors

Gogo
grandmother, Granny

ibutho
regiment
(plural: amabutho)

inkosi
chief

inyanga
traditional healer
(plural: izinyanga)

Iwombe
the name of one of
Dingiswayo's regiments

Nkosi
respectful way of
addressing a chief

Nkosi yami
my chief

isangoma
diviner, traditional healer
(plural: izangoma)

umuthi
traditional medicine

umuzi
homestead/settlement
(plural: imizi)

yebo
yes

PRONUNCIATION

Zulu contains some sounds which are not used in English, but it uses letters from the English alphabet to represent them.

CLICK SOUNDS: C, Q, AND X

c To make the sound of the letter 'c', suck the tip of the tongue against the palate, just behind your front teeth and then pull it away. This makes a soft click sound. It is like the sound English speakers use to show sympathy ('tsk').

q To make the sound of the letter 'q', suck the tip of the tongue against the roof of your mouth, and then pull it away suddenly. This makes a hard click sound like the sound English speakers use to imitate the sound of a horse's hoof on hard ground.

x To make the sound of the letter 'x', suck the side of the tongue against the inside of your cheek, and then pull it away suddenly. This makes a click sound like the one that English speakers use to call a horse.

English uses the sound 'th' which is not used in Zulu.

th When you see the letter combination 'th' in Zulu you can pronounce it like the English letter 't'. For example, 'Mthethwa' can be pronounced as 'Mtetwa'.